To Uncle Joe
with best
wishes
from

RED IN VERSE

*Rhyming Tributes to the Liverpool Greats -
from Liddell to Gerrard*

PHIL DOMINGO

Phil Domingo works as Assistant Principal at Kingsthorpe College, Northampton.

For any shared memories e-mail:
phil.domingo@kingsthorpecollege.org.uk

Also by Phil Domingo:

'Songs from a Liverpool Childhood: a Narrative of Life in the Sixties'

First Published 2009 by Countyvise Limited.
14 Appin Road, Birkenhead, CH41 9HH

Copyright © 2009 Phil Domingo

The right of Phil Domingo to be identified as the author of this work has been asserted by him in accordance with the Copyright, Design and Patents Act 1988.

British Library Cataloguing in Publication Data.
A catalogue record for this book is available from the British Library.

ISBN 978 1 906823 24 5

For Peter

This book is dedicated to the memory of two Postal Officers and stalwarts of the Main Stand:

Vincent Domingo and Graham Crofts

'Motherwell? Yes thanks'

Acknowledgements

Thank you...

To Vinton for drawing John Barnes and Ian Rush.

To Natalie for helping me draw Kenny Dalglish and the little kicking footballer logo (started as John Toshack but couldn't get the head right!). Thanks Nat for also encouraging me to draw the others. Everything is possible!

To Colin Armitt for helping me get the original manuscripts typed.

To Bill Shankly - the architect of the greatness described in these pages.

Contents

RED IN VERSE

Everlasting Love

Subject - L.F.C

Apologies to "The Love Affair"

Open up your eyes, then you realise
Here I stand with my
Liverpool F.C.

From the very start
Deep down in my heart
Never for to part
Liverpool F.C.

For over forty years
Through the songs and cheers
The laughter and the tears
Liverpool F.C.

Tales of happy days
Glory "sans pareil"
At Anfield and away
Liverpool F.C.

At times they made us curse
With the occasional reverse
Enjoy this "Red in verse"
Liverpool F.C – Everlasting Love for ever.

(Written when we were a club, not a brand.)

Boots of Thunder

A tribute to the late great Billy Liddell and the man who
worshipped him from the Kop.

When I was born in fifty-five, the greatest hero then alive?
The Scotsman with the boots of thunder, which tore
      defences well asunder.
Upon the wing he played the game, and Billy Liddell was
      his name.

It was an April Saturday – Liverpool at Leeds away,
When midwives did deliver me, at Oxford Street maternity.
"A baby boy – we've got a lad," my mother did inform my
      dad,
"I'm thrilled to bits but can I tell you that Billy Liddell's just
      scored two.
Against Leeds United's centre-half, none other than the
      great John Charles".
The earliest words I learned to say, not nursery rhymes, no
      "curds and whey".
But "Liddellpool, Hip, Hip, Hooray!"
And so we were to live our lives, from three o'clock till
      quart' to five,
Endless Saturdays to endure, dependent on a football
      score.

Upon the mantelpiece at home, there stood a picture quite
      alone,
Cloven hair-style, parted down the middle, above the
      craggy smile of...Billy Liddell.
Of Billy's praises dad did sing, at centre-forward and the
      wing,

"William Beveridge", he would enthuse. "Played for Great
	Britain with Matthews.
What an honour – and what is nice, the only two selected
	twice!".

It's Manchester City in the cup, we're two-one down, time
	nearly up,
An equalising shot then flew, just as the final whistle blew.
So Billy's goal was disallowed, in spite of protests from
	the crowd.
	(and one man in particular!).

At Goodison with Uncle Stan, who is an Evertonian,
	(no known cure)
Billy L. and Johnny Evans took my dad to seventh heaven.
As Liverpool from Division Two humiliated boys in blue.
Come on Toffees what's the score? Blue boys NIL Red
	men FOUR.

Now my own heroes come and go, comparisons they start
	to flow.
"What about Roger Hunt, St. John?"
"No match for the chosen one."
"And Kevin Keegan does he impress?"
"No candle held to the Scots' Express".
"And Kenny the Aristocat?"

--- Silence ---

"Philip, please don't make me answer that".

It's 1980 in the rain, near the Players' Entrance before a
	game.

3

Just as we are to take our place, my dad spots a familiar
        face,
"Look it's Billy, there's no doubt".
"Say hello dad but please don't shout".
"Hello Billy how are you?"
He smiled politely, "Fine thank you".
But do you know what is really sad?
...He never recognised my dad. (Why should he?)

Billy Liddell

*Absolute icon to an older
generation, not least to
Vincent Domingo*

As Billy approaches St. Peter's gates, a crowd has
        gathered and guess who waits.
Right at the front to greet the man? It's my old dad his
        greatest fan.
And he will take Billy by the hand and show him to his seat
        in the heavenly stand.

My big regret right to this day is never seeing Billy play.

Shelter from the Storm

Subject - Bill Shankly

Apologies to Bob Dylan

It seems like another lifetime, one of toil and mud.
Honesty was a virtue, hard work did you good.
He came to us from Huddersfield, and took it by the horns.
'Come on' he said, "let's go and take the football world by storm".

Though hardly great in stature, a giant on the scene.
He built the club from nothing, and so, too, a great team.
He preached the simple virtues, of keepball and hard work.
He had no time for phoneys, or those who sought to shirk.

He valued the supporters, and seemed to understand.
That everything was possible, if we walked hand in hand.
In the moments of great glory, the first thing he would do,
Was raise his hand out to the Kop and say, "this one is for you".

He brought the club promotion back in 1962.
Once more in the top flight, nothing else would do.
The fans, they stormed on to the pitch, and wallowed in the mud.
They chanted, "Liverpool cha cha " the feeling was so good.

And soon we were League Champions with Roger and the rest
A team equipped to terrify Europe's very best
The sixties ' boys are legends,but meanwhile off the field
The seeds were being carefully sewn for an even greater yield.

He won the cup for Liverpool, back in 1965
The first time in our history, it was great to be alive
He stood there on the Wembley turf, raincoat in one hand
A finger pointing to the sky, acknowledging the fans.

And so to 1966, we're champions once more
The team by now is legendary, admired and adored.
We're feared throughout Europe, great names are filled with dread,
At the thought of being drawn against a team dressed all in red.

I asked him for an autograph, one day at Burnley's ground,
He accidentally dropped the pen, "I'm sorry son" he growled.
I was utterly dumbfounded, and had to disagree,
That this person whom I'd idolised, should apologise to me.

The new team of the seventies, was geared for success,
With Keegan as the talisman, they continued to impress.
The UEFA cup, the League again, and Wembley once more –
The "party pieces" final of 1974.

On a summer's day of that July, the football world stood still,
Paralysed and traumatised by the news that mighty Bill,
Had decided on retirement, it left us so forlorn.
He'd had enough and looked to find some shelter from the storm.

In the wake of his retirement, it was hard to understand,
That he fell out with this great club, the finest in the land.
Try imagining a love ravaged and ripped torn,
And the fans caught in the middle had to walk on through the
        storm.

When Bill fell ill in '81, his demise was all too fast,
How could it be that the Great Shankly would be an icon of the
        past?

When it comes to "precious memories", the feelings are so
      warm,
They sustain us in the bad times, like giving shelter from the
      storm.

Love minus hero? No limits!

Bill Shankly

"I wanted to create a bastion of invincibility"

Hail Glorious

Subject - Ian St John

Refrain

Hail Glorious Ian St John
Dear saint of our team
When you played in Europe
We were the cream
Your name it is a legend
Emblazoned in red
Because of that goal
Scored from your sacred head

Poem

In the beginning was the word
And the word it was St John
And it thundered from the Kop
Across the park to Everton

Short, stocky, skilful
The Saint he was the boss
He scored the longest goal in
History when he netted from Hunts Cross

About to be crowned Champions
Back in April '64
The Kop was singing Beatle songs
Game with Arsenal was in store

Tucked in behind Arrowsmith
And Roger Hunt as well

The Saint appeared in the box
To fire past Furnell

The floodgates now were open
The Bridge was falling down
Liverpool scored four more times
New Champions were crowned

Thompson bagged a couple
Alf and Roger each scored one
But the toast at Anfield on that day
Was to a certain Ian St John

He held the line for Scotland
This greatest son of Motherwell
He mixed vision with aggression
He gave defenders hell

Back to Wembley '65
With the game in extra time
Leeds United in the rain
And St John in his prime

Bremner had just equalised
Roger's opening nod
Then came that timeless moment
When a Saint became a God

The ball was played to Callaghan
Who sprinted for the line
The cross was near perfection
The header was sublime

Ian St John

His neck was stretching backwards
To meet the ball head on
The roar was heard for miles around
HAIL GLORIOUS ST JOHN

Noble Knight of "Goal Born"

Subject - Sir Roger Hunt

Refrain
Sir Roger Hunt ,Sir Roger Hunt
EE AYE ADDIO Sir Roger Hunt
Echoes
Roger Hunt is wonderful
Roger Hunt is wonderful
Full health, full of go
Full of vigour
Roger Hunt is wonderful

Poem
This noble son of Golborne
The first Knight of the Kop
Whose goals from all directions
Took Liverpool to the top

With left or right
Or with golden head
From point blank range
Or far out instead

His repertoire knew no bounds
No player could be bolder
The first to feel
The Kop's sword of steel
Placed upon his broad shoulder

First game of the season
Back in August '64

Opponents they were Arsenal
Who could ask for more?

The cross it came from Cally
I see it to this day
The first goal ever televised
On Beeb's Match of the Day

A super volleyed cross shot
That arrowed to the top
Of Roger's favourite goal net
"The one before the Kop"

The '65 Cup Final
Had gone to extra time
A mazey run by Stevo
Finds Gerry near the line

A driven ball across the goal
The Kop begin to roar
As Roger stooped to conquer
In opening the score

And so to the biggest night
Of every Liverpool fan
The Euro semi-final
Against Inter of Milan

The F A Cup paraded
You have to know the truth
A roar so loud was registered
That we nearly lost the roof

Sir Roger Hunt

The European Champions
Visibly shook with fear
Invited back to Italy
To the tune of "Santa Lucia"

The atmosphere electric
The Kop was filled with glee
As Roger's volleyed opener
Rocked the pride of Italy

St John scored in the second half
And Cally pulled a stunt
But the Emperors of Milano
Were slayed by Roger Hunt

Easter Saturday, '68
It's Sunderland at home
The ball fed in from Thompson
Nearly forty yards from goal

13

The game was drifting aimlessly
The Kop was melancholy
He flicked the ball above his head
Turned and hit a volley

So sweet and true and wonderful
And that is just a summary
And those who saw it shan't forget
And neither will Montgomery

The London press disparaged him
Mocked his ungainly style
Labelled him a 'workhorse'
Attacked with their bile

They seemed to ignore that it was (Geoff) Hurst
Who took the place of Jim(Greaves)
But Roger kept on scoring goals
It never got to him

Roger Hunt had greatness
His record tells us so
At home, abroad and World Cup
He graced the stage we know

Colossus

Subject - Ron Yeats

I'll tell you of a Football Team
And Liverpool is the name
They've won the cup, they've won the league
They're the finest in the game
We've got the greatest skipper
Any manager could employ
Lets drink, six crates to Big Ron Yeats
Bill Shankly's pride and joy
        (Stan Kelly)

Ron Yeats

Shankly's Colossus

Signed from Dundee United back in 1961
To make a spine for our great team
Along with Ian St John
He was the great Colossus who Shankly doted on
It was Bill' s request
To invite the Press
To walk around Big Ron

15

As you can well imagine he was peerless in the air
His legs were telescopic and appeared from nowhere
It was always so uncanny
He was always so aware
To heed the call
And win the ball
Eradicate the scare

Reprise

Tell me who is the player with the black curly hair
Who stands at the head of your band
Seven feet is his height
With some inches to spare
He looks like a king in command
Well Ron Yeats is his name
The finest skipper in the game
And the greatest of heroes to a man
(Stan Kelly)

Feet of Wonder

Subject - Peter Thompson

Bought from Preston in '63
In the mould of Tom Finney
When this man was old the ball
His feet of wonder did enthrall

Peter Thompson

His dribbling skills were unsurpassed
He kept the full backs well harrassed
Like a matador to a bull
He'd taunt defenders to the full

Now he's here, then he's gone
The elusive pimpernel "Thompson"
And just for fun it seemed back then
He'd go and beat his man again

This often would frustrate the crowd
"Once is enough" they'd shout out loud
"Ole, Bravo", show him who's boss
But Peter get the ball across

We found out later that this man
Worked to orders; worked the plan
To keep the ball, to bring relief
To give his team-mates time to breathe

At Villa Park in '65
Fed by St John, he did contrive
To taunt poor Chelsea, make them doubt
And turn Marvin Hinton inside out

With his defenders in a trance
Bonetti never stood a chance
And so the mobile Kop assembly
Knew that it was next stop Wembley

He played for England once in a while
This dribbling wizard from Carlisle
It was a mystery to his fans
How he rarely figured in Ramsey's plans

It can't have been his rate of work
With sleeves rolled up he'd never shirk
And with his talent, he would scheme
To always benefit the team

Latterly he moved inside
To prompt Steve Heighway running wide
My final tribute and I feel it wants one
Was to name my son after Peter Thompson (which I did)

Viva Bob Graham

Apologies to "The Equals"

The Kop   Viva Bobby Graham
Viva Bobby Graham
Bobby Graham
Viva Bobby Graham
Viva Bobby Graham
Viva Bobby Graham

Scored a hat trick on his debut
Aston Villa they all sure knew
They had seen a finishing show for free yeh
Bobby Graham and his goal machine
Everybody knew they'd seen
A sensation, a sensation know what I mean

At the G Pit one November
Sandy's own goal I remember
Bobby's through hoping he can make it
     three yeh
Took the ball round Gordon West
Scored a goal of the very best
A sensation, a sensation
Hear what I say

Viva Bobby Graham etc

Scored an early goal against Chelsea
Went to trap a ball and then see
What was on, but he didn't get a chance to
     do so

19

Bobby Graham broke a leg you see
He came back, but he ceased to be a
      sensation
know what I mean

Viva Bobby Graham etc

Reds Remembered (Part One: The Boys of '62)

How we remember Ronnie Moran,
Who re-appeared against Inter Milan
To play his part with style and class
To evoke memories of the past
He became a coach of high esteem
The sergeant major of our team
And in our history he holds a place
This celebrated Bootroom Ace

And Gordon Milne I do recall
Whose distribution of the ball
To Saint and Roger was so keen
He was the heartbeat of the team
He had awareness and great vision
To gain him England recognition
I'd like to recognise in rhyme
The greatest right half of his time

Now Jimmy Melia he could play
I remember to this very day
A tricky schemer,a skilful one
Who linked up well with Hunt ,St.John
But he moved on when Shanks did deem
To need more power in the team
Later on our Jim was found
Disco dancing in Brighton town

Refrain
"My memories are very dim of Kevin Lewis, Leishman, Jim
        (Furnell)

I'm sure you will forgive my crime,I was only seven at the
time."

And Kevin Lewis was to score
In the opening Derby a 2-2 draw
A goal scoring winger who lost his place
To Peter Thompson no disgrace
Furnell and Leishman played their part
To take Division Two apart
And even so they soon gave way
We...salute them to this day.

And almost as an afterthought
We cast our minds to Alan A'court
Who played alongside Billy Liddell
Allowing him to move to the middle.
And for England did he earn selection
When we were in the second section
And greatly do we owe a debt
To this tricky little outside left

The 850 Special

Subject - Ian Callaghan

The 850 Special running down the line
The 850 Special mocking Father Time
850 appearances – a phenomenon
The 850 Special Ian Callaghan

A model pro' a manager's dream
This crucial member of the sixties team
The greatest servant known to any club
18 years of toil, sweat and love

A debutant at seventeen
Replacing Liddell in the team
Undaunted by this awesome task
He did precisely what Shankly asked

A direct winger early on
Supplying crosses for Hunt and St John
And later he was employed greatly
To make the goals for Tony Hateley

In tandem with the tricky Thompson
He worked the flanks and lots of games won
Opposing full backs filled with fear
As Cally and Thompson stepped up a gear
Opposition stretched and grilled
"If Thompson doesn't get you, Callaghan will"

Leeds United's Willie Bell
In '65 was given hell

The Scottish full back filled with dread
As Cally's cross met St John's head

And later on that Tuesday night
Faced with Facchetti and Italy's might
Inter Milan fell for the trick
As Cally converted a (well) worked free kick

As the sixties team retired
A midfield general was required
To link the old guard with the new
To show the youngsters what to do
Shankly thought, "I know the man
I'll convert Ian Callaghan"
Who made the transition without a seam
To become the heartbeat of the team
So now there's two parts to the story
Sixties greats and seventies glory

Against the Arsenal in '72
It's Frank McClintock and his crew
A five goal thriller was in store
Up popped Cally on the edge
Of the Arsenal box and made a pledge
To chip keeper Wilson, poor old Bob
And so he did with an audacious lob
Executed perfectly
To fill the Kop with mirth and glee
Storey and Simpson had converged
To pressure Cally who emerged
Between the two so skilfully
It's Arsenal two, Liverpool three

Stoke at Anfield, score one-one
Clock is ticking time almost gone
Cally received a pass with thanks
For the last ever goal against Gordon Banks

In Rome's Olympic stadium the 25th of May
Callaghan and Heighway sent McDermott on his way
Amid the glory that was Rome
All heroes to a man
None more than the veteran, Ian Callaghan

From Wembley 65 to Roma 77
Inter and St Etienne, the nights of Kopite Heaven
The most legendary occasions over a twelve year span
Feature the phenomenal Ian Callaghan

Ian Callaghan

The Mighty Inside Left

Subject - Tommy Smith

Tommy Smith

With a number ten upon his back,
But playing deep alongside Yeats,
He appeared against Anderlecht
A youthful titan among the greats.

So looking for an Inside Left,
The Belgian Champions were bemused
And soon they were to be bereft,
Outfoxed by this Bill Shankly ruse.

His tackling soon became the stuff
Of legendary anecdote,
For one so young he was so tough,
He took each game (and some opponents) by the throat.

Sure he could tackle, that's no myth,
Keeping forward lines at bay.
Lest we forget that Tommy Smith
Was one hard man, BUT HE COULD PLAY.

As big Ron moved to pastures new,
A great new leader was required,
To motivate Shanks' latest crew,
To domineer, cajole, inspire.

So Tommy was the obvious choice,
To lead into the new decade,
And Kopites to a man (and woman) rejoiced,
Delighted by this accolade.

The Championship returned once more,
With UEFA cup in '73,
Among the many cups galore,
In our UNRIVALLED history.

And so to the twenty-fifth of May,
Picture the glory that was Rome,
A corner kick from Steve Heighway,
And guess who soared to head it home?

It's mighty Tommy from the back!
Who with his head he did connect,
In supplementing the attack,
And turning up at……..INSIDE LEFT !!!!!

Silent Knight

Subject - Chris Lawler

Traditional Christmas Carol

Silent Knight, stealthy Knight
Like a thief in the night
Appears surprisingly in the attack
60 odd goals from position full back
Secret weapon from deep
Opposition asleep

Silent Knight, stealthy Knight
At the back keep it tight
With his partner Gerry "Crunch" Byrne
Wingers don't know which way to turn
Full back pairing sublime
Contrasting styles back in time

Silent Knight, stealthy Knight
To the Kop's great delight
European defences can't rest
Liege, Juventus, Honved Budapest
Slain by Lawler from deep
Opposition asleep

Chris Lawler

Silent Knight, stealthy Knight
Creeping up out of sight
In the Derby trailing by two
Heighway and Toshack stage a rescue
Then Chris Lawler appears
Everton in arrears

Reds Remembered (Part Two)

How we remember Willie Stevo,
A quintessential Scottish hero,
A classy half-back with great vision,
Who passed the ball with great precision
Shanks salvaged him from Glasgow Rangers,
When emigration was a danger,
His mazey dribble in '65,
Brought the Final tie alive.

How we remember Gerry Byrne,
A crunching tackle at every turn,
He broke the barrier of pain,
And never once did he complain.
Who could ever forget that night,
Parading the cup, oh! What a sight!
With Gordon Milne his injured mate,
Another of the Shankly greats.

And so too we recall Geoff Strong,
Bought from Arsenal to join the throng,
Shankly's Mr. Versatile,
Where'er he played, we liked his style.
His injured knee he did ignore,
To devastate the Celtic hordes,
As Cally's cross he leapt to meet,
To doom the Scotsmen to defeat

Crazy Horse

Subject - Emlyn Hughes

When Shankly saw that younger blood
Would help his vintage team
He looked to Blackpool for a boy
Who ran all day it seemed

He took the treasured number "six"
Of classy Stevenson
The fans at first were quite perplexed
But saw the boy could run

With flailing arms and surging runs
He took the game by force
His youthful zest soon won the fans
Who named him "Crazy Horse"

In a midfield role or at left back
He always did enthuse
Without, within you always win
When you've got Emlyn Hughes

The FA Cup in sixty-nine
Matched us with Tottenham
He took the ball from Mullery (who packed in)
A famous sortie he began

From half-way line he made the run
The Spurs defence just backed away
He hit a cross shot with great force
And became the hero of the day

Jennings could only stand and watch
The ball which flew into his net
"Tony the Tiger he was good
 but this one was the best goal yet"

'Mighty' Emlyn Hughes

*Still the only British footballer
 to hoist every trophy in club
football*

I clearly remember, his brace at Goodison (72/3)
The joy we shared, the great delight
As he slayed Everton
Shankly made him captain in the middle seventies
By which time he was a centre back
A role he played with ease
He became the national skipper
A job he did with pride
A more patriotic captain has never led the side

Every big club trophy
He hoisted and brought home

At Molyneux, Bruges and Anfield, Wembley and Rome
A younger red support may wonder
Who was he like?
It's déjà vu cos Emlyn Hughes
Was Steven Gerrard's prototype

That European Trophy so cherished by the fans
Really looked magnificent in Emlyn Hughes' hands

The Ballad of Tommy & Clem

Subject - Tommy Lawrence & Ray Clemence

Apologies to Georgie Fame

Tommy & Clem a pair of super keepers
Who doubled up as sweepers
In the Shankly era
Tommy was big
Of ample constitution
(who) became an institution
In the sixties team

Bridge

He knew a lot about flying
And the Kop could see
That opponents were sighing
Foiled by the bare handed feats
Of the Liverpool man in green
Providing a line of defence
Then the envy of every team

Link

Then one day
Shanks knew things had to change
He took himself over
To see Scunthorpe play
And travelled back with Super Ray

When Clem replaced Tom
It was a smooth transition
In the Liverpool tradition

34

It was kept internal
And quite very soon
On him we were dependent
This ex-deckchair attendant
With the golden hands

Tommy Lawrence

*Bare handed and brave keeper from
the sixties*

Phil - D.

Ray Clemence

*Added more value than any
other player*

Phil -D

Bridge
More athletic than Tommy
Ambidextrous too
We remember so fondly
The numerous saves

In significant games
When he saved the day
We can't forget the formidable debt
That we owe to Ray

Exemplar
One fine night, we remember in Rome
The save from Bonhoff in the nick of time
The European Cup came home

Born to Play Wide

Subject - Steve Heighway

Apologies to Steppenwolf

When we saw him running
His devastating wing play
Like a top express train
His name is Stevie Heighway
Oh! Boy he's gonna make it happen
Full back in his wake
Bob Wilson at the near post nappin'!

One-nil no mistake
And so the final came alive
Early on in extra time
He could fly so fast
Defence high and dry
Born to play wide

High steppin action
Zooming past his full back
Crossing from the bye line
Feeding Keegan, Toshack
One time he took a flick from Toshack
Right in to his stride
McFaul never saw it coming
Magpies open wide

Steve Heighway

So now the score now two-nil
Because Steve swooped to kill
He can fly so fast

37

The cup home and dry
Born to play wide

The bigger the occasion
The better Stevie Heighway
We're on our way to Roma
By every route and byway
Steve spots that McDermott's running
Through ball in to space
First goal against Moenchengladbach
My god what an ace
And from Steve's corner kick
To the head of Tommy Smith
Who soared so high
We all touched the sky
Born to play wide

Heard of Steven Gerrard?
Heard of Michael Owen? Who?
You've heard of the Academy
It's reputation growing

Footballing production line
What a boost for the England team
New stars all the time
England's Munich holiday (2001)
Due to the work of Steve Heighway
They can fly so high
Almost touch the sky
He was their guide
Born to play wide

The Quartermaster Scores

Subject - Brian Hall

Traditional Song

He shot he scored and all the Kopites roared.
Brian Hall, Brian Hall

A BSc from university
Brian Hall, Brian Hall

In seventy one he shattered Everton
Brian Hall, Brian Hall

Bridge   My eyes are dim but I still see
              A ball hit on the half-volley
              That took us all to Wem-b-ley

He shot he scored and all the Kopites
Roared Brian Hall, Brian Hall

Bridge   He may have been quite small and slight
              He did the business on the right

Here, There and Everywhere Else

Subject - Kevin Keegan

Apologies - The Beatles

Once a young man sat on a bin
Wondering if he would feature at all
If he'd receive a call
Then a debut in front of the Kop
I witnessed the goal that started it all
A player who would enthral

Bridge
Who ever thought he would be
A famous sporting icon of the seventies
A player of such great ubiquity
For he was here, there and everywhere
Here, there and everywhere

Soon he was king of the Kop
The bond between us seemed
Strong that's for sure
We thought it would endure
Then once he decided to go
The reasons for leaving
Just stuck in your throats
"A challenge" not just bank notes?

Bridge
We can remember still
How we won the cup and thwarted Newcastle

We thought he'd stay for life and it was a bitter pill
When he was here, there and everywhere (else)

Once he was on Top of the Pops
"Head over Heels", "It ain't easy" he'd sing
He wasn't exactly "Sting"
Then he grew tired of his hair
"So hard to manage, in need of a Perm"
Hopefully not long term

Bridge
We can remember well the final show in Roma
Vogts was given hell
A foul inside the box and Kevin Keegan fell
He was here, there with Curly Hair!

49th Street Bridge Song

Subject - Sir Bob Paisley

Apologies - Simon & Garfunkel

Slow down you're going too fast
Got to make the season last
Treat it like a marathon
Hark the words of "Gunner" Paisley

Here's a man seems so ordinary
Achievements Extra-ordinary
Flat cap, cardy, slippers too
Don't be fooled by "Gunner" Paisley

Phil-D

Sir Robert Paisley

Nine successive trophy years, including three European cups. No Knighthood brings the honours system into disrepute.

Nine successive trophy years
Home and Europe held no fears

42

Greatest ever Football boss
What's the name? Oh! "Gunner" Paisley

"What's the secret?"
It's not great"
A balanced side that concentrates
"Dead straightforward honestly"
The famous words of "Gunner" Paisley

They honoured him eventually
With no more than an OBE
Deserved a Knighthood certainly
Sounds so right "Sir Robert Paisley"

Ray of Gold

Subject – Ray Kennedy

Apologies – "Sting", Eva Cassidy

And he came to us from the Arsenal
Where he'd been a fearsome rival
Where he'd played up front
And a double won
As a centre-forward bold

Shankly's last great act
Was to sign this man
After winning the cup final (74)
Paisley soon sussed out
That he could adapt
To a crucial midfield role

Prompting from the left
Joining with attack
Sure his play was devastating
And the honours flowed
And the trophies shown
Around the pitch of Anfield Road

The great Ray Kennedy

Remember how and when
Against St. Etienne
He gave a ball of great precision
For a super sub name of Dave Fairclough
To score a very famous goal
Lest that we forget
That great left foot strike

44

When he scored at Bayern Munich
How it set us up
Another Euro Cup
Would return to Anfield Road

In the great big games
Like the Cup Finals
We were always optimistic
Cos we always knew that among our crew
Was the mighty Ray of Gold

After every game he would feel so tired
He was utterly exhausted
No one ever guessed there was something wrong
We were shocked when we were told

He had been struck down by disease so cruel
It affects his every movement
And we hope and pray that the mighty Ray
Will soon find his Ray of Gold

We're so thankful now for the part he played
The player of his decade
For his vital goals, visionary role
And his passes made of gold.

Those who saw him play
Recall the subtle way
He would activate his team-mates
You cannot overstate how this all time great
Bestrode the pitch at Anfield Road

Hit the Net Mac

Subject – Terry McDermott

Apologies to Ray Charles

Chorus
Hit the net mac
Terry's gonna score, gonna score, gonna score
Hit the net mac
Listen to the Kopites roar

We bought him from the Geordie team
A player of low self-esteem
Paisley told him "Yes You Can"
You're more than just a "ragbag" man

Chorus

A midfield player from Kirkby town
Whose goals would bring the whole house down
The opening strike in Rome
A legend in every home

Chorus

Terry McDermott

*Double player of the
year 1980*

46

Oh woman, oh woman please treat me right
We're going out on the town tonight
And the toast is Terry Mac
He sent those Moenchens so sad back

Chorus

Derby semi-final at old Maine Road
Lawson standing slightly out of goal
Should a seen him hurtling back
As he was lobbed by Terry Mac

Chorus

Tottenham in Seventy Eight
Finished a move that was so great
He started it from the back
Number Seven headed in by Terry Mac

Chorus

A wonder goal at White Hart Lane
Cross field volley killed the game
In 1980 have no fear
The Double Player of the Year

Chorus

The greatest team goal ever seen
Devastated Aberdeen
With Razor and Kenny so slick
Made ole Pizza Face sick

Chorus

Addendum

Subject – Steve McMahon

Man United Eighty Eight
We need a goal it's getting late
A shot to storm a barn
Released by Steve McMahon

Hit the net mac
Steve's gonna score gonna score gonna score
Hit the net mac
Listen to the Kopites roar

South End Man

Subject - Jimmy Case

Apologies to Neil Young

There was a rumour sent by word of mouth
Of a great talent in the suburbs south
A South End Man, Pride of Holly Park
Had a bite worse than any bark

South End Man

South End Man lived on my estate
Destined to be an Anfield great
South End Man was a shooting ace
South End Man's name is Jimmy Case

South End Man

Bridge   Jimmy Case scored at Wemb-ley
                Turned and volleyed over Step-ney
                Thought we might go on to victory
                How wrong   How wrong

                South End Man King of Allerton
                Jimmy Case Scourge of Everton
                South End Man why did you have to leave?
                Prematurely, it made us grieve

                South End Man

Bridge II   Jimmy Case he made the South End proud
Such a favourite with the Anfield crowd
When he left us our heads were bowed
How wrong   How wrong

Jimmy Case

Reds Remembered (Part Three)

How we remember Peter Cormack,
Who prompted Keegan and John Toshack,
Whose silky skills we all agreed,
Gave the team its subtlety.
Who could forget how Pete,
A Scotsman with the twinkling feet,
Made the Wembley Kopites roar,
With his display in '74.

And Philip Thompson we remember,
He of the Kop – a paid up member,
Who fulfilled every Kopites' dream,
To play for his beloved team.
He partnered Emlyn at the back,
And made a raincoat of a mac! ('74).
We'll not forget the sight as he,
Raised that cup in Gay Paree! ('81).

Thrilling us Softly

Subject - Kenny Dalglish

Apologies to Roberta Flack

He came from Glasgow Celtic
A well established name
To replace Kevin Keegan
In the Hall of Fame
We wondered just how he would satisfy our needs
Winning our hearts with his magic
Weaving a spell all around
Thrilling us softly with his skill
Ripping the heart from opponents
Thrilling us softly … With his skill

He took a pass from Souness
At Wembley Seventy Eight
He clipped the ball so deftly
Perfect in its weight
The ball it sailed so sweetly
In to the Belgian net
Sending the cup back to Anfield
Champions of Europe again
Thrilling us softly with his skill
Ripping the heart from the Belgians

He formed a lethal pairing
With Ian Rush of Wales.
They were so devastating
All the heights were scaled
They would destroy defences

52

With combination play
Passes of subtle precision
Putting young Rush through to score
Prompted by Kenny's great vision
Thrilling us softly with his skill

And then one day at Chelsea
He took it on his chest
He hit a sumptious volley
     Of the very best
     He led us to the double
     As player manager
     Winning our hearts with his magic
     Leading the club to success
     Thrilling us softly with his skill
     Ripping the heart from opponents
     Thrilling us softly

Kenny Dalglish

Red Divinity

Phil and
Nat.

He put a team together
Some say beyond compare

With Barnes and Peter Beardsley
Aldridge he was there
They played such total football
Tom Finney eulogized
"Better than even Brazilians"
Footballing skills so sublime
They are a team in a million
Greatest of all time, of all time
Thrilling us softly, in our time

One afternoon in Yorkshire
The worst we ever spent
Our people led to slaughter
By the establishment
Who did we then all turn to
To assuage the pain
He was our natural leader
It happened to him over night
He was the one that we needed
To lead us adroitly through our pain
Lead us adroitly

Then almost two years later
The strain it took its toll
So much depended on him
And unrealistic goals
Resisting great persuasion
He bowed out from the scene
Leaving us wonderful memories
Of big Trophies hoisted galore
Thrilling us softly with his skill
Ripping the heart from opponents
Thrilling us softly

Caesar (His was no disgrace)

Subject Graeme Souness

Apologies to Yes

Yesterday_a legend played
A Scottish midfield ace
Caesar's passing ,McDermott's glory
Kennedy and Case

Sure his tackling it was toothy(his words)
But don't forget the flair
Remember please his distribution
Way beyond compare

Orchestrator Midfield General
Pulling all the strings
Passes of such perfect vision
So regal, like a king

Euro Final going nowhere
Bruges in Seventy Eight
Picked out Kenny through congestion
Pass of perfect weight

'84 it was his swan song
To bring a treble home
Olympic stadium
Caesar's Palace – Emperor of Rome!

Irrespective of his record
Managing the team
It's the player we remember
And hold in such esteem

Graeme Souness

Imperious and complete as player and captain

Oh Where are they Tonight?

Subject Alan Hansen and Mark Lawrenson

Apologies to Bob Dylan

There was a tall centre half
With the skill of Beckenbauer
From Partick Thistle he did sign

He was a master of space and time
And his skill was so sublime
Gliding in a style so divine

There was an Anglo-Irish ace
With electrifying pace
From Preston originally

In this partnership of old
His praises were extolled
Far and wide so vigorously

Any nobody could disguise
They were more than streetwise
As they played with their heads and their hearts

And though many strikers tried
They were soon to be denied
And never were the pair pulled apart

Bridge
Now they're both on the telly
On Match of the Day

Telling modern players
The proper way to play

Oh to wind back the clock
And turn back the page of a script
That nobody could write

Oh where are they tonight?

……In some studio.

Mark Lawrence

Top pundit, better defender

Alan Hansen

*Credibility as a TV pundit
drawn from immaculate
playing record*

Aerial Majesty

Subject - John Toshack

Apologies to the Men of Harlech

John Toshack

Stevie Heighway's always running
John Toshack is always scoring
When you hear the Kopites roaring
Toshack is our King

Our love affair with Cardiff started
Long ago, when Toshack parted
To play for Liverpool wholehearted
Toshack is our King

In the air there was none better
Great provider and goal getter
Followed Shankly to the letter
Toshack is our King

In the Derby we are trailing
Two-one down we look like failing
Aerial Majesty prevailing
Toshack is our King

Telepathy made in Heaven
With his partner, "number seven"
You remember that bloke Kevin
Toshack is our King

Great team player not a loner
Took the knocks, not once a moaner
And he scored in Barcelona
Toshack is our King

The Listener

Subject - Alan Kennedy

Apologies to Walter De LaMare

"Ya ba da ba doo" cried the Kopite
When the ball was launched high and long
By the left back bought from Newcastle
To join the Anfield throng

"What are you doing?" asked Souness
Who looked at him aghast
"We like the ball played to our feet"
As Kennedy looked downcast

"I come from a world of listeners
And I know you want the ball played more
So it runs along the surface of Anfield's grassy floor."

And very soon he was established
Integrated to our style
But he continued to play with gusto
Guaranteed to raise a smile

And he was christened Barney Rubble
A character of Flintstone fame
And soon he was to join the legends
For his contribution to great games

Alan Kennedy

Phil-D.

Namesake Ray took a throw in
At Parc des Princes '81
From nowhere did appear our Barney
With the Real defence just looking on

"What's he doing there?" thought Souness
As Barney took it on the up
He glided the ball past the Keeper
To land the European Cup

One thing they say about lightning
Is that it never ever does strike twice
But in the '84 penalty shoot out
The final throw of the dice

"Somebody send for Barney"
As Hansen couldn't bear to watch
So our hero approached the Roma goal
And the penalty was despatched

"Tell them, I came, saw and conquered"
We're back in heaven once again
The European Cup is lifted
Said a voice from the world of men

One thing we like about Barney
In many ways he's just like us
But he scored a goal in four Cup Finals
And never understood the fuss

Reds Remembered (Part Four)

I can see David Johnson to this day,
He played the game the Liverpool way,
He chased and harried, ran and ran,
Like a mad dog after the milkman's van.
How we remember in '78,
A diving header oh so great,
To deny the Gladbachs once again,
The Euro' Cup soon to retain.

And Davey Fairclough we recall,
The greatest super sub of all.
A label he would always hate,
But Davey's impact was so great.
Clearly we remember when,
He scored against St. Etienne,
He took a ball played o'er the top,
And buried it before the Kop.

Who could ever forget Phil Neal,
The full back with the goal appeal.
And when of width there was a lack,
He'd come attacking from the back.
Who could ever forget in Rome,
Those penalties well driven home.
When it required nerves of steel,
We'd always turn to Philip Neal.

How we remember Joey Jones,
Who munched the Gladbachs when in Rome.
A Welshman who we did adopt,
He had a rapport with the Kop.

With forearm bare and fist raised high,
And attitude of ne'er say die.
Motivated by the cause,
And driven by the Kopite roars.

Proud Mersey

Subect - Ronnie Whelan

Apologies to Credence Clearwater Revival

Once an Irish midfield player
Prompted from the left in his early days
Scored some winning goals
In two League Cup Finals
Picked out Ian Rush sent him on his way

Ronnie Whelan

*So easy to write about, so
difficult to draw*

Bridge
Whelan keep on running
Proud Mersey keep on winning
Ronnie Whelan, Whelan will deliver

Kenny moved him to the middle
To break up the attacks and to win the ball
Linking with McMahon, Johnny Barnes and Beardsley
Ronnie tackled tough
Ever standing tall

Bridge
Whelan keep on running
Proud Mersey keep on winning
Ronnie Whelan, reelin' in the trophies

Goals You Need - It's Rush

Subject - Ian Rush

Apologies to "The Beatles"

The greatest striker ever known
All the scoring records blown
His earlier career was when
Level was offside
Amazing
All you need is Rush

The game is heading for a draw
No one looks like they will score
Striking like a Cobra
In minute eighty nine
It's Rushie
All you need is Rush
…Rush is all you need

He was the scourge of Gwladys Street
Twenty plus with head and feet
Shattered the record
Of the mighty Dixie Dean
It's easy
All you need is Rush

In 86 and 89
He broke their hearts
Time after time
He won those finals with a brace
Of goals so fine

It's easy.......
All you need is Rush

In '92 we all gave thanks
He finally scored against the Mancs
And we were looking on
The brighter side of life
Remember
All your need is Rush

A Cup Final statistic
Ian Rush has scored in SIX
This is a record that will
Last eternally
-Eternally-
All you need is Rush

Remember back in '88
We had a team already great
When Rushie came back to us
So we killed the fatted calf
The Prodigal
All you need is Rush

VINTON

Ian Rush

I was driving in my car
The news it reached me from afar
Got so excited, nearly crashed the bloody thing
It's easy
The return of Rush

Refrain
He's coming home, he's coming home
Rushie's coming home

-(2)-

Reprise

I heard the news today oh boy
About the return of a Prodigal
It blew my mind so in my car
I had to go to the pub and
Have a celebratory jar

Refrain

The greatest Welshman ever born
Some say John Charles but I am torn
Between this legend and Flintshire's favourite son
Not easy
All you need is Rush

Reprise

Nothing compares,
Nothing compares to Rush

Mr Magic Wingman

Subject - John Barnes

Inspiration – Bob Dylan

Chorus
Hey Mister Magic Wingman
Play a cross for me
Beardsley and Aldo are in waiting
Hey Mister Magic Wingman
Dribble well for me
The red and white supporters will be following you

Remember down in Rio back in 1984
He dribbled through to score
Brazilians on the floor
A star was born and Dalglish salivating
He could have gone most anywhere
His talent to parade
The memory can't fade
He cast his dancing feet our way
And before the Kop his play was devastating

Chorus

Take me disappearing to the golden memory
Of John Barnes' trickery
Received the ball half way
Held QPR at bay
And before the Kop
He left young Seaman groping
He danced beneath the Anfield sky

His technique so sublime
He mastered space and time
We never lost our grip
Upon our championship
And we made a bond that
Never would be broken

John Barnes

VINTON

With Beardsley and Aldridge
A Triangle of Gold
Attacking play so bold
And twice within five days
Notts Forest blown away
Left Cloughie in reflective rumination

And later on as Father Time
Diminished his great pace
He never lost his grace
He took a central role
And prompted from the soul
For Rush and Fowlers' sharp anticipation

Chorus

And if you see vague traces
Of a controversial view
I'll argue through and through
This master of the ball
Was the greatest of them all
Although for England he could be frustrating
His courage was unquestionable
When under scrutiny
He kept such dignity
And Wembley's racist hordes
Were manfully ignored
His head held high
His feet communicating

Chorus

Reds Remembered (Part Five)

Who could ever forget Big Jan?
A mountain of a Danishman.
A hulking guy with dancer's feet,
Whose passing gave us all a treat.
Who could ever forget how Jan,
Came roaring forward with great elan.
And take that game with Everton,
Right by the throat – a double won!

And Stevie Nicol what a star
At full back or at centre-half
Size 14 boots upon his feet
In spite of this he was so neat
He could dribble, turn and shield
He played for Scotland in midfield
He played with verve, he played with style
The Eighties Mr. Versatile.

And Brucie Grobelaar acrobat
A parrot sewn into his hat
He went all wobbly at the knees
And Roma missed their penalties ('84)
He got poor Hansen out of trouble
And we went on to win the Double ('86)
And from his goal he'd often stray
This maverick son of Zimbabwe

And we recall ole Smokin' Joe
The part he played, the debt we owe
Encouragement and great advice
He proved that winners could be nice

He coached the team to great effect
Commanding always great respect
For '84 we hold him dear
The FIRST of our great treble years.

Do you remember Sammy Lee?
He prompted Rush in '83
Who spurred on by the Park End roar
Went on to score 'The Famous Four'.
And Sammy closed Falcao down
When we prevailed in Roma's ground ('84).
He fetched for Souness skilfully,
Unselfish, unsung, Sammy Lee.

Recall Craig Johnston, Socceroo.
He skipped around, his aim was true.
"Slow down Craig", exhorted Bob,
"A steady tempo is the job."
A Predator in '86,
He thwarted Mimms between the sticks,
And helped to burst the 'bluenose bubble'
When Rush was ready at the Double.

Steve McManaman

Apologies to T.S. Eliot

Chorus   McManaman, McManaman
There's no one like McManaman
A purveyor of the rounded ball
A dribbling phenomenon

In need of inspiration
League Cup Final '95
He took on Bolton by himself
And brought Wembley alive
A brace of virtuoso goals
You've never seen such flair
When we need a genius
McManaman was there

Chorus

Up at Parkhead, Glasgow
We need a two-two draw
Till Macca ran from his own box
So memorably to score
The Tartan Army was aghast
That he would even dare
It needed something special
McManaman was there

Chorus

Now Houllier's done a brilliant job
To resurrect the side

But they sometimes cannot
Break down teams
Cos no one's playing wide
I know who'd do a job for us
A thought I cannot bear
Just when we could do with him
McManaman's not there

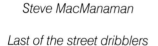

Steve MacManaman

Last of the street dribblers

McManaman, McManaman
A team mate of the great Zidane
Astella Vista, Adios
Senor Steve McManaman

Deus

Subject - Robbie Fowler

Apologies - Writer of Church Hymns

Seek ye first the Kingdom of God
And his sweet left foot
That was the downfall of many many teams
Alleluia etc

He very soon was the darling of the Kop
How they worshipped him
How he was supported
Through his troubled times
Alleluia

He was the one to whom we turned to most
Through the barren years
One seven one goals
In three hundred games
Alleluia

Remember back to 1995, How he slayed the Mancs
Twice Schmeichel beaten by a Fowler brace
Alleluia

Remember fondly his majestic lob
Against Birmingham
"Worthy" of winning
Any Cup Final
Alleluia etc

Remember the great goal, against Alaves
How we were convinced
It had won the game at last
Alleluia

God doesn't live by bread alone
He wants first team games
To show the world
His devastating skill
Alleluia etc

How can we live without our number 9
And his skills sublime
We even loved the plaster on his nose
Alleluia etc

Robbie Fowler

*A fellow Toxteth boy. He gained
divine status on the Kop.*

La Merseysaise

For Gerard Houllier

Allons les enfants de la Mersey,
Les jours de gloire sont revenus,
Nous sommes menés par le professeur de football,
Et son équipe de bon esprit vaillant,
Gerard Houllier, Hurrah Houllier.
Marchons! Marchons! A travers la tempête,
Plein d'espoir dans le coeur.

Allez les champions de Gerard Houllier,
Nous surveillons un ciel doré,
L'armée rouge va réussir en Europe.
Comme les hèros braves de nos époques passées,
Gerard Houllier, Hurrah Houllier.
Marchons! Marchons! A travers la tempête,
Avec bonheur dans le coeur.

*Written after the treble win in 2001. A time of great optimism
when Gerard could do no wrong.*

Tommy "Swiss" and the Mighty Finn

Subject - Stephane Henchoz and Sami Hyypiä

Apologies to Bob Dylan

Houllier was building hopes and dreams
Once again a bastion, an invincible team
We were so excited every girl and boy
"When Sami Hyypiä gets here
Everybody's gonna jump for joy"

Come on without, come on within
You'll not see nothing like the Mighty Finn.

He and Stephane Henchoz like the Berlin Wall
Best defensive barrier in British football
They perform like heroes, giants among men
With Sami H and Stephane,
We're gonna rule the world again

Come on without etc.

Sami finally left us after ten great years
His last game was emotional
He was choked with tears
His goal against Juventus was a joy to see
When I think about Sami Hyypiä
That's the one I see

Sami Hyypiä

Come on without etc.

The Anfield Boat Song

Subject - Michael Owen

Poem deleted - as is the memory.

Immigrant Song

Subject - Jon Arne Riise

Preceded by Robert Plantesque wailing

Aaaaaaaaaaah etc.

He comes from the land of the ice and snow
From the midnight sun where the hot springs flow
His shirt above his head, in everyway a red
Destroyer of the bluemen, Chelsea and the Mancs
And when he takes a free-kick he leaves them feeling
        dead sick
'Oh hell he is going to score'

Starman

Subject - Steven Gerrard

Since age eleven he's been part of L.F.C
Tutored and nurtured at the red academy
Led by Steve Heighway who was heard to say

"He's a starman,dominates midfield,
A demon in the tackle, never see him yield,
Such a starman Huyton born and bred
Coveted by many but remains Forever Red"

Hear the Kopites singing, hear the Kopites singing
Hear the Kopites sing his name

He stars for England and now it's history
A goal in Munich led to victory
And Dieter Hamman he was heard to say

"Ich heise Hamman, ich spiele in midfield
Mit der Starman, we Germans we all reeled
Such a starman for greatness he was bred
Er ist ein starman and I'm glad he's still ein red"

Hear the Kopites singing etc

Within the era of the foreign superstar
Steven Gerrard can outshine them all by far
Feared by his rivals who've been heard to say
"Bloody hell Steven Gerrard's playing"

One night in Turkey, getting beat 3-nil
Our hopes in tatters, such a bitter pill
Who did we turn to, to drag us through the mire?

Starman, soaring through the air
Destination goalwards, he will take us there
Starman, the Liver bird in flight
Never knows he's beaten, such a fearsome sight

Hear the Kopites cheering, Now Milan are fearing
Hear the Kopites sing his name

Steven Gerrard

We All Dream

Subject - Jamie Carragher

In the town where I was born
Lives a man who we all rate
And his service to the cause
Turned a good lad into great

We all dream of a team of Carraghers etc.

And he bears the torch passed down
It's a legend not a myth
From Phil Thompson, Emlyn Hughes
And the Mighty Tommy Smith

We all dream etc.

And that night in Istanbul
Jamie stood for all to see
As he gave his very all
To see us home to victory

We all dream etc.

Is it just his lionheart
That makes this player one to fete?
Or his talent very rare
Unrivalled gift to concentrate?

Jamie Carragher

Concentration personified

We all dream etc.

(Mama Mia) It's Fernando

Subject - Fernando Torres

The boy they call El Nino
Has come to join our ranks from sunny Spain
Let's celebrate with vino
The fact that he will score important goals
For us again
And the lad they call Fernando is crowned a king
And before the Spion Kop will reign

Bridge

There was something in the air that night
Our star shone bright, Fernando
He was scoring goals for you and me, for victory, Fernando

The Lions of Istanbul

They travelled in their thousands for the 25th of May
We've known for many years it's a very special day
      (Rome 77)
To get there was imperative and every stunt was pulled
A car was sold, a 'sickie' thrown, to get to Istanbul
Told they shouldn't go there, it's very dangerous
They charmed the birds down from the trees beside the
      Bosphorus
And then into the stadium a swirling sea of red
To dominate the Ataturk and fill Milan with dread
"We're down here by the Bosphorus
To reclaim what belongs to us"

Kick off

Maldini netted in the First (minute)
Matters couldn't get much worse
Then Hernan Crespo bagged a brace
And we were facing big disgrace
At half time we anticipate
The routing of a club once great
You wouldn't give a toss for us
As we perished by the Bosphorus
We would settle for four nil
Anything more just brought a chill
Olympiakos I did muse
But no one else would share my views
"An early goal would do perhaps"
"A.C Milan will not collapse"

Surrounded by his grieving Reds
Rafa alone did keep his head
He said "I've got a cunning plan
I'll bring on Didi, Herr Hamman
I'll not bring on a fresh attacker
'Cos don't forget you're playing
Kaka (couldn't be any more
Cacker)
Objective one just get a goal
And Didi he will fill the hole"
As A.C celebrate their 'win'
Stevie Gerrard feeling grim
Says "50,000 of our firm
Have paid good money so hard earned
They're still singing clear and loud
Let's get out there and do them proud"

And Hamman did Milan subdue
As Gerrard led the charge anew
And mighty Carra at the back
Blanked Shevchenko in attack
Jon Arne Riise on the left
Twice taken cross, the second deft
And Stevie met it with his head
The early goal like Rafa said
And Stevie signalled to the crowd
"Give it loads and give it loud"
And they sucked in our glorious past
And blew it out with such a blast
That Milan quivered just like Juve
"We're on the march, we're in the groove"
And Didi passed to Vladimir
Whose sweet struck shot cost Milan dear

A Smicer goal? You wouldn't bet
It sailed into the Milan net
Right now who is your money on
As Gerrard plundered with aplomb?
Milan were in a state of shock
As Stevie stormed into the box
"He keeps a coming mama mia
He has no nerves he has no fear"
As Stevie was about to score
Gattuso tripped him to the floor
If Xabi puts this pen away
We equalise "Oh make my day"
But Dida dives down to the right
And stops the shot we think "Oh there's a shame"
Xabi Alonso did not fret
And put the rebound in the net

The world of football was enthralled
By the greatest comeback of them all
Then Liverpool just hung on in
Exhausted by their will to win
Milan comeback, they are so strong
And purposeful they're back on song
Shevchenko's through, he's bound to score
But enter Dudek fear no more
And every commentator raved
About Jerzey Dudek's double save
And extra time it came and went
And Liverpool were surely spent

So penalties we must endure
We've got a German he must score
Our final hope it rests upon

The Polish nation's number one
And Carragher was observed on telly
"Do like Brucie – legs of jelly"
And sure Italian nerves were shot
As their first pen was skied aloft
The second, Jerzey he did stop
To the approval of the Kop
Then Didi, Djibril, and Vladi
Put away each penalty
Cut to Sevchenko he came up
To keep Milano in the cup
The world's top striker if you please
Thwarted by our Jerzey's knees

And every Red in every place
Can wear a smile upon the face
A decade in the wilderness
Is now wiped out by this success
And every Kopite still alive
Can boast about the Famous Five
And this assertion say it loud
The first big cup won by a crowd
In Istanbul and back at home
Our boys they never walked alone

Oo Eez Deez Fairclough?

First published in the fanzine 'Red All Over the Land' 2002

It is of course Jubilee year. As Liverpool supporters prepare to celebrate the Silver Jubilee of their club's finest moment I thought I'd kick off proceedings with a personal anecdote from 77.

During the long hot summer of '76 I had qualified to teach English. In direct contrast to today the teaching jobs' market was very tight especially for those offering 'mainstream' subjects such as English.

French had been my second subject at college. The course had been brilliant including a six-week placement near Strasbourg. I had enjoyed teaching French on teaching practice but although I had all the theory in my head, I knew my spoken French was insufficient to sustain a career.

I wanted to speak French fluently. I needed to live there a while. One of my lecturers was a native of Provence and had good contacts. I approached her to see if she could find me work. When she got back to me she said there is a post but it would suit a teenager, not a qualified teacher. It was a job as an in-house care assistant in a children's home near Avignon. It would involve a lot of domestic duties with the opportunities to help the children with their English in the evening.

The pay and conditions were lousy board and lodgings plus a bit of spending money but I was undeterred. As a student I was unused to money. I would make do to become bilingual. I flew down to Marseille in the middle of August. It was of course 1976 and I remember not having to acclimatise too much the other end, such was the heat in the UK on departure.

I soon learned that to live and work in a foreign country (even one in Western Europe) on your own is a very tough thing to do. The job was even more unsuitable than anticipated but I was determined to tough it out.

I endured long periods of isolation living in a little tiny village of 900 people where the bar closed fifteen minutes before I finished work in the home each evening. My one release was training and playing for the local village football team. However I could only represent them one weekend in two, due to my work commitments.

Throughout the loneliness and homesickness, my oxygen was the reciprocal correspondence with my friends and family. My mum would write from our home in Garston every week and my girlfriend (later to be my wife) from college fortnightly. However, once a week my dad would ring me from his work on a Monday night, with a match report from the previous Saturday. I might already have known the score, might have even seen the goals on telly, but dad's match report was a lifeline.

"They sing 'Liverpool are magic', Philip and I have to say they are," he would whisper, not wishing to be found out. Basically I had chosen to be abroad in the season that the very good team I had watched clinch the championship at Molyneux, crossed the threshold to greatness. Delighted as I was with the results, this "magic" that I could not witness made the homesickness worse.

In addition to his phone calls, dad would send a bundle of newspapers each week including the *Football Echo*. I wanted to be involved in the debate so I would write to the letter's page whenever I had something to say.

After Liverpool had drawn St. Etienne in the quarter-final of the European Cup it had caused great excitement throughout the home and the village. I was known as

"Keegan" in the village purely because I was English, no other resemblance, and everybody wanted to talk to me about the forthcoming tie. In the absence of a dominant national team (how times change) the whole of France got behind their premier club. I had seen the Saints overcome PSV Eindhoven live on telly and was impressed. They had some of the best players in Europe, the midfield master Bathenay, tricky winger Rocheteau and the awesome Argentine defender Piazza.

I wanted to transmit the excitement felt in France to everybody at home. I wrote a letter, which included the phrase "OO EEZ DEEZ Fairclough" alluding, to our secret weapon for the tie. I didn't think anymore of it perhaps they might print it in the Saturday letter's column.

One evening circa February '77 my dad phoned out of the blue. "You've really done it this time. The *Echo* has interviewed your mother about your 'Andy Warhol fifteen minutes of fame'."

We are the only Domingo family in the city, so my relatives had to put up with the ensuing interest which must have irritated them - all except my mother of course who told everybody in Garston market, interested or not.

The *Echo* asked me to write a pre-match feature about the game insisting I was "Our man in St. Etienne." The reality was I was living in the little tiny village of St. Etienne Du Gres many kilometres to the south.

And so to the game. My dad managed to get me a ticket for the "away" leg in France. For me it would involve a two hour coach ride from Avignon. I managed to obtain "passionate leave" from work and my boss, in an uncharacteristic bout of sensitivity to my interests, even gave me a lift so I could buy the coach tickets.

OO EEZ DEEZ FAIRCLOUGH?

Don't worry Pierre lad —you'll see, warns Phil

★ Carrying the flag for Liverpool in the heart of the St. Etienne camp with dedicated Scouse fervour is 21-year-old Phil Domingo, a Garston lad with a neat turn of phrase and massive optimism about Liverpool's chances in the forthcoming European Cup quarter final against the French champions, writes Michael Charters.

He is a regular writer to the Echo on Liverpool matters—his mother says he has been contributing to our letters 'column since he was 11.

Son of Mr. and Mrs. Vincent Domingo, of Garfourth Road, Garston, Phil has been working in a St. Etienne orphanage for the past six months, brushing up his French language as part of his studies towards taking a Bachelor of Education degree. In between speaking French and teaching the children at the orphanage, he seems to be spending most of his time telling the locals how good Liverpool are. His letter explains:

Having, for the last six months been in St. Etienne preaching the invincibility of Keegan, Toshack and Co., the thrilling European

Cup draw has assumed enormous personal significance. The result of the tie stands to make me either prophet or fool of the year.

Being in France is rather like being in a pub full of Evertonians on the eve of a derby match. I am forced to carry the banner, single handed, and on evenings when the wine flows like the Red Sea, I have no doubt made some outrageous forecasts.

I must tell folk back home what we are up against. Sport in France is St. Etienne. The whole population wants to see the game and, in Cup Final fashion, I wait for my ticket on a promise of a promise.

"Les Verts" area bigger unifying factor out here than either Bonaparte or Beaujolais.

Phil Domingo

I have no fear though. The French Press and club apies alike have made the common mistake of judging Liverpool in the midst of their usual January recession.

From a theoretical, spectatorial point of view, the simplicity and directness of the Liverpool game lulls them into false security that we will be difficult adversaries, but beatable.

However, like many would-be tactical connoisseurs before them, the

So on the afternoon of the second of March I made for Avignon on my moped, which I would leave at the flat of an English mate. I would stay here in the remaining hours of the following morning after the match. As I approached the coach bound for St. Etienne, I was draped in red and white flag and scarves last worn at Molyneux '76. I will never forget the expressions on the faces of the "Avignon Greens" as they realised this red Englishman would be a fellow traveller.

Remember this in the seventies. Imagine doing this in England and not being torn apart limb from limb. Not possible. I knew in France it would be safe. In fact, I was more than safe I was welcome.

Once they recovered from my effrontery, the 'Green' supporters were wonderful. We shared food and drink, banter and songs. They sang 'Allez les Verts' not to be out done I gave a rendition of YNWA and a full Kop karaoke. I think they were genuinely appreciative that my team meant just as much to me as theirs did to them. I was really excited at the prospect of seeing this new magic Liverpool for the first time that season.

The game was a thriller. We played well. Heighway hit the post but we went down late in the game to a Bathenay chip. I was proud of the boys, the result obviously retrievable. In some ways perhaps for me it was the ideal result bearing in mind the journey home.

I was able to watch the return leg on TV at the home with the older children who by now were developing Liverpool accents. Luckily, it was on a Wednesday, the one mid-week night when any of us, staff or children were allowed to watch telly. The match which we saw in black and white was the stuff of legends. My dad was locked out and had to view the game in the Holt pub.

To our enduring delight, Davey was sent on, took a perfect ball from 'Ray of Gold', and buried it in the Kop goal just as we faced elimination on the away goals rule. I had become a 'five minute soccer prophet'. I went potty. I survived at the home 'til April. The moped got destroyed in Corsica (another day another tale), but not before I had watched the first leg semi final victory against FC Zurich in some bar in Ajaccio.

I returned home to Garston penniless, having borrowed the train fare, but I was reasonably fluent in French, which impressed nobody in Garston British Legion. The decision to go to France had been a good one as it has given me a meal ticket for life to this day.

For my contribution to their paper, the *Echo* gave me two free tickets for the Kop to see the Zurich home leg. I was impressed at the time. I took my little sister, the now, famous mid-wife Gillian Maysmor of Woolton. The Editor of the *Echo Sports*, a Mr Kelly invited me to lunch to 'discuss things'. When I rang to arrange a date, he was out. He never returned my call and I was too shy to pursue it.

I met David Fairclough last year before the Rotherham Cup game and explained his part in my 'Andy Warhol' experience'. To my astonishment he remembered that publicity as clearly as I had. He was very friendly and I was thrilled when he told me my article was in his scrapbook. It's in mine.

Three of Us

In Jupiter Street (unadopted) we parked our car (c. 1967)
And boys appeared from near and far.
"Can I mind it Mister, there'll be no catch.
 It will still be here after the match."

We'd start to walk the golden mile,
Excitement building all the while.
We'd dodge the cars at Breck Road lights,
The road to Anfield in our sights.

And so we're now on Walton Breck,
And past the big pub on the left.
A father walking with his lad
The proudest time for any dad.

We see the signs for Walker's Ales,
The smell of onions now prevails.
The step now quickens, pulses race.
Fortnightly ritual taking place.

By now the road it straightens out,
Souvenir sellers all about.
And desperate fellows here and there,
Asking if "there's any spares?"

Pedestrian traffic all one way,
To Anfield on a big match day.
And behold it's Mecca, eyes aloft.
The silver roof of Spion Kop.

Volume rises on our approach,
More fans arrive by bus, by coach.
We plan to meet at the D:E:R (telly shop)
Then separate and say "tara".

Dad takes his seat in the Kemlyn Road.
I make for the Pen, but he'll never know,
That I'll sneak to the Kop, unless I get hurt,
And get passed down to sit on the dirt.

And after the match once more we'd meet,
And make our way back to Jupiter Street (unadopted).
He'd ask some questions,he'd ask a lot,
He'd ask me about the view from the Kop.

35 years later.........

I make that journey from time to time ,
Now I'm the dad and the lad is mine.
But I feel a presence in my bones,
And sense that we don't walk alone.

In the centenary stand ....

The turnstile clicks for only two,
But could it be that we know who
Has come to join us – quite discreet,
As we sit near his former seat?

Old Kopites never die, they just float around Anfield on match days.

97

Glossary - The Reds

Strong Geoff, p.30
Thompson Peter 'Twinkletoes', p.13, 17-18, 22, 23
Thompson Phil 'Kopite', p.51, 84
Toshack John, p.29, 37, 51, 59-60
Whelan Ronnie, p.65
Yeats Big Ron, p.15-16, 26, 27

An objective indicator of the impact and influence of a player or manager could be the number of times they get a mention. Little surprise therefore to see Mr.Shankly in the lead. Notice also that St. John, Sir Roger, Kenny, Stevie Heighway and Gerrard appear frequently and, no matter how we feel about the manner of his departure and subsequent aftermath, so does Kevin Keegan. The stats don't lie, do they ?

Phil's all time 11

Clemence

Smith(capt.)   Hansen   Lawrenson   Nicol

Peter Thompson Souness Gerrard   Barnes

Dalglish   Rush

The bench: Reina, Carragher, Hughes, Heighway,
St.John,Torres, Fairclough

Glossary 2 – The Others

Bathenay Dominic (St Etienne, France), p.93
Banks Gordon (Leicester C., Stoke C.), p.25
Bell Willie, (Leeds U.), p.23
Beckenbauer Franz (Bayern Munich, W.Germany), p.51
Bonhoff Reiner (B.Moenchengladbach, W.Germany), p.36
Bonetti Peter (Chelsea), p.18
Brown Sandy 'own goal' (Everton), p.19
Charles John (Leeds U., Juventus, Wales), p2, 68
Clough Brian (Manager of Derby C., Leeds U., Notts
    Forest p.70
Crespo Hernan (A.C Milan, Chelsea, Argentina), p.86
Dean William Ralph 'Dixie' (Everton), p.66
Dida (A.C Milan, Brazil), p.87, 88
Fachetti Gianni (Inter Italy), p.24
Falcao (F.C. Roma, Brazil), p.65, 73
Finney Sir Tom (Preston N.E.), p17, 53
Gattuso (G.Rangers, A.C Milan, Italy), p.88
Greaves Jimmy (Chelsea, A.C Milan, Spurs, West Ham
    U.), p.14
Holland Stan, Evertonian Uncle (Haileybury All Stars with
me and Michael), p.3
Hinton Marvin, (Chelsea), p.18
Hurst Sir Geoff (West Ham, Stoke), p.14
Jennings Pat (Spurs, Arsenal, Rep. of Ireland), p.31
Kaka (A.C Milan, Real Madrid, Brazil), p.87
Kelly Stan (Liverpool folksinger and wit), p.15, 16
Lawson David (Everton), p.47
Maldini Paolo (A.C Milan, Italy), p.86
McClintock Frank (Leicester C., Arsenal, QPR), p.24
McDonald Malcolm (Fulham, Newcastle U.), p.51
McFaul Liam or Willie (Newcastle U.), p.37

Mimms Bobby ('South' Everton), p. 73
Mullery Alan (Fulham, Spurs, Brighton H.A.), p.31
Piazza Oswaldo 'The Beast' (St. Etienne, Argentina), p.92
Ramsey Sir Alf (Manager of England), p.18
Rocheteau Dominic (St.Etienne, France), p.92
Schmeichel Peter (Man U., Denmark), p.76
Shevchenko Andriy (A.C.Milan,Chelsea, Ukraine), p.88, 89
Seaman David (Birmingham C., QPR, Arsenal), p.69
Simpson Peter (Arsenal), p.24
Storey Peter (Arsenal), p.24
Stepney Alex (Millwall, Chelsea, Man U.), p.47
Tiger Tony (The Kellog's Frosties X1), p.32
Vogts 'Dirty' Bertie (B.Moenchengladbach, W.Germany)
     p.41
West Gordon 'Gwladys' (Everton), p.19
Wilson Bob (Arsenal, Scotland), p.24
Zidane Zinedine (Real Madrid, France), p.75